Bible reflections
for older people

The Bible Reading Fellowship
15 The Chambers, Vineyard
Abingdon OX14 3FE
brf.org.uk

The Bible Reading Fellowship (BRF) is a Registered Charity (233280)

ISBN 978 1 80039 041 6
All rights reserved

This edition © The Bible Reading Fellowship 2021
Cover photo © Tatiana Rodriguez on Unsplash

Acknowledgements
Scripture quotations marked with the following abbreviations are taken from the version shown. Where no abbreviation is given, the quotation is taken from the same version as the headline reference. NIV: The Holy Bible, New International Version (Anglicised edition) copyright © 1979, 1984, 2011 by Biblica. Used by permission of Hodder & Stoughton Publishers, a Hachette UK company. All rights reserved. 'NIV' is a registered trademark of Biblica. UK trademark number 1448790. NRSV: The New Revised Standard Version of the Bible, Anglicised edition, copyright © 1989, 1995 by the Division of Christian Education of the National Council of the Churches of Christ in the United States of America. Used by permission. All rights reserved.

Every effort has been made to trace and contact copyright owners for material used in this resource. We apologise for any inadvertent omissions or errors, and would ask those concerned to contact us so that full acknowledgement can be made in the future.

A catalogue record for this book is available from the British Library

Printed and bound in the UK by Zenith Media NP4 0DQ

Contents

About the writers

Roger Combes has served in a variety of parishes in London, Cambridge and Hastings. Before retiring, he was archdeacon of Horsham. He and his wife, Christine, now live in Crawley, West Sussex, where Christine is the gardener and he cuts the grass.

Tony Horsfall is a freelance trainer and retreat leader based in Yorkshire. His BRF books include *Deep Calls to Deep* (second edition, 2021), *Resilience in Life and Faith* (2019, with Debbie Hawker), *Servant Ministry* (second edition, 2019) and *Spiritual Growth in a Time of Change* (2016). He also contributes to BRF Bible reading notes *New Daylight*.

Ro Willoughby has been writing and editing Christian resources for many years. She has recently been licensed as a lay minister at St Chad's Woodseats in Sheffield, where she is engaged in ministry with people of all ages. It is a great joy that she now lives close to her children and grandchildren, as well as close to Bakewell and Chatsworth House – although she hasn't yet received an invitation to the ball!

Angela Tilby worked for the BBC as a producer of religious programmes for 22 years. Ordained in 1997, she became a tutor at Westcott House in Cambridge. After some years as a parish priest, she moved to Oxford as diocesan canon of Christ Church Cathedral. She writes for the *Church Times*, broadcasts frequently on Radio 4's *Thought for the Day* and is a canon emeritus of Christ Church Cathedral.

From the Editor

Welcome to this new collection of Bible reflections.

'Dance like nobody's watching' is a line from a popular fridge magnet quote. Often attributed to Mark Twain, it's sadly unlikely that he ever said it. The encouragement to be yourself, without fear of judgement, is almost certainly much more recent, but the advice is still sound.

Dance classes for older people are increasingly popular, thanks to the Royal Academy of Dance's Silver Swans initiative. The programme enables older learners to take part in ballet classes, whatever their previous experience. The creators know that dance isn't just about fitness and balance and being able to touch your toes; it's an expression of something deep and enduring within ourselves which cannot be put into words.

People across the world were profoundly moved last year when a video of Marta Cinta González, a Spanish ballerina with advanced Alzheimer's, went viral. The film begins with a slight, blank-eyed Marta, hunched in a wheelchair. Then, as her carer plays Tchaikovsky's 'Swan Lake' in her headphones, we watch in awe as Marta is transformed back into the ballerina she once was, and clearly still is.

The psalmist exhorts the faithful to praise God with dancing and with music. Even if it's only tapping a toe or gently swaying to the tune of a favourite hymn, that's still dance and still an expression of our love for God, in which he delights.

God bless you.

Using these reflections

Perhaps you have always had a special daily time for reading the Bible and praying. But now, as you grow older, you are finding it more difficult to keep to a regular pattern or find it hard to concentrate. Or maybe you've never done this before. Whatever your situation, these Bible reflections aim to help you take a few moments to read God's word and pray, whenever you have time or feel that would be helpful.

When to read them

You may find it helpful to use these Bible reflections in the morning or last thing at night, but they work at any time of the day you choose. There are 40 reflections here, grouped around four themes. Each one includes some verses from the Bible, a reflection to help you in your own thinking about God, and a prayer suggestion. The reflections aren't dated, so it doesn't matter if you don't want to read every day. The Bible verses are printed, but if you'd like to read from your own Bible that's fine too.

How to read them

- **Take time** to quieten yourself, becoming aware of God's presence, asking him to speak to you through the Bible and the reflection.

- **Read** the Bible verses and the reflection:
  - What do you especially like or find helpful in these verses?
  - What might God be saying to you through this reading?
  - Is there something to pray about or thank God for?

- **Pray**. Each reflection includes a prayer suggestion. You might like to pray for yourself or take the opportunity to think about and pray for others.

One another

Roger Combes

A teacher of even very young children wants to get them interacting and stimulating one another (in a good way!). The conductor of a choir trains them to listen to each other. A business leader builds a team which will spark and support one another. A sports coach looks for 'team players', not just individual stars. An army commander needs soldiers who will be committed to each other through thick and thin.

Similarly, Jesus of Nazareth insisted on followers who would be fully committed to each other. Famously he said they must love one another. They were to be 'one another' people.

The little phrase 'one another' comes several dozen times in the New Testament. Writers Paul, John, James, Peter and the writer to the Hebrews, like Jesus, all use it and call on Christian disciples to be mutually supportive of each other.

These reflections look into this 'one another' living, which is a mark of Christ's people locally and universally. It comes in many forms but is always practical. Sometimes it feels more like giving and sometimes it feels more like receiving, but in practice it is both. Christ challenges us, and blesses us, through one another.

John 13:14, 34–35 (NIV)

Wash one another's feet

'Now that I, your Lord and Teacher, have washed your feet, you also should wash one another's feet... A new command I give you: love one another. As I have loved you, so you must love one another. By this everyone will know that you are my disciples, if you love one another.'

We all know the story of the good Samaritan, in which Jesus teaches us to 'love your neighbour as yourself'. This is different. This is the story of the foot-washing teacher, where Jesus does a roleplay on how we should love our fellow disciples. The standard seems even higher: not 'as you love yourself,' but 'as I [Jesus] have loved you'.

Jesus and his disciples come in for a meal. The hands-on task of washing everyone's feet from the grubbiness of the road falls to a junior servant. Except that here, Jesus, who is the head of the group, does it himself. They are all shocked. But Jesus insists this is to be the norm for them. Such acts of practical, self-effacing care for one another will be the sign that they belong to him.

Can you think of Christian people who act like this to help you? And are there some ways in which you show similar practical care to other followers of Christ?

■ **PRAYER**

Praise God for those in the church who give lifts, do gardening, collect from school and in other practical ways care for their fellow disciples.

Romans 12:5, 10 (NIV)

Put one another first

In Christ we, though many, form one body, and each member belongs to all the others... Be devoted to one another in love. Honour one another above yourselves.

A handful of very small children are released into the garden, where there is a gleaming new slide to play on. 'Me first! Me first!' they chorus. As we get older, we learn to control, or at least disguise, the 'me first' impulse. 'Women and children first!' is the call at the life-boats. Hopefully, the men comply. In the same vein, parents in desperate poverty across the world tend to feed their children before themselves.

We could compare Christians, members of the church, to members of a good team. They are fully committed to each other. They put one another first. They work for each other and assist each other. They give credit first to one another and to the team as a whole before taking any themselves.

In church life, as in life in general, it is all too easy to ignore or marginalise people, especially those who are different from us. Sometimes it is children who need to be put first in our church thinking, or deaf people, or students, or refugees, or people in their workplace, or ex-offenders, or people hurt by local issues. 'Honour one another above yourselves,' says the apostle.

■ PRAYER

Lord Jesus, you treated everyone as important and took them all seriously. Help me to do the same. Amen

Hebrews 10:24–25 (NIV)

Spurring one another on

Let us consider how we may spur one another on towards love and good deeds, not giving up meeting together, as some are in the habit of doing, but encouraging one another – and all the more as you see the Day approaching.

A professional tennis doubles match is usually entertaining. The players seem to enjoy it, but they take it seriously as well. Have you noticed how they keep coming together throughout the game to have a quick exchange on tactics, or simply to encourage each other for the next point?

The Jewish Christians reading these verses needed to spur one another on. They were probably feeling a bit isolated, having left the 'buzz' of temple worship for the much smaller fellowship of Jesus' followers meeting in someone's home. Isolation can demotivate.

But the Christian life was never meant to be lived alone. Surprising as it may seem, you encourage others just by being with them in church. Like the tennis players, we stimulate each other as we come together, and faith and love grows. Someone may spur us on into some activity for Christ that we would never have dreamt of doing, and we benefit as a result. Perhaps if you are largely cut off from others, could you arrange to meet online or by phone to be alongside someone else?

■ **PRAYER**

In Luke 22:32, Jesus says he prayed that Peter would strengthen his fellow disciples, which he did. Let us pray that we may do the same.

1 John 1:5b–7 (NIV)

One another fellowship

God is light; in him there is no darkness at all. If we claim to have fellowship with him and yet walk in the darkness, we lie and do not live out the truth. But if we walk in the light, as he is in the light, we have fellowship with one another, and the blood of Jesus, his Son, purifies us from all sin.

'One for all and all for one' was the famous motto of Alexandre Dumas' *The Three Musketeers*, such was the bond between them. This spirit of belonging to each other makes a real difference to a group's performance. It improves their resilience, motivation, ambition, cooperation and mutual trust. Who would not want that?

Christian fellowship is like that, only much better. It is the bond we have with Christ and our heavenly Father – and with each other. In common with believers across the world, we all share in the life of Christ. Such sharing binds us together and strengthens us on many levels.

In order to enjoy this fellowship, our way of life needs to be 'in the light', because God is light. This means no concealing of our wrongs from God and no deceiving of other people; rather, we live our life in accordance with the light God has shown.

■ **PRAYER**

The grace of our Lord Jesus Christ, and the love of God and the fellowship of the Holy Spirit be with us all evermore. Amen

Colossians 3:12b–13 (NRSV)

Bear with one another

Clothe yourselves with compassion, kindness, humility, meekness, and patience. Bear with one another and, if anyone has a complaint against another, forgive each other; just as the Lord has forgiven you, so you also must forgive.

The church buildings were having a maintenance blitz, and I was a volunteer. In charge was Paul, who asked me to measure several small, cracked panes of glass so they could be replaced. This I did carefully, but when the new glass arrived, all the panes were two centimetres too small. I had messed up badly. I felt awful and apologised profusely. Paul was busy, but he said cheerily, 'Don't worry!' and gave me another job. I was impressed at his treatment of such a mistake-prone volunteer, and was grateful to him.

Does anyone suffer fools *gladly*? The apostle Paul simply says in a context of compassion and kindness that we should 'bear with one another' and 'forgive each other'. He seems to recognise that even within the church there are difficult people we have to get on with. And if we remember the occasions we have made things difficult for other people, it makes it easier to forgive others when they irritate us.

Jesus had to cope with difficult or foolish people, and he bore with them with understanding and patience. Unforgettably, as he was being crucified, he said, 'Father, forgive.'

■ PRAYER

Lord Jesus, bless the people I see often, especially any who have wronged me or whom I just find difficult. Amen

Ephesians 5:18b–20 (NIV)

Singing together

Be filled with the Spirit, speaking to one another with psalms, hymns, and songs from the Spirit. Sing and make music from your heart to the Lord, always giving thanks to God the Father for everything, in the name of our Lord Jesus Christ.

Where were you when you first sang, 'Jesus loves me, this I know' or 'To God be the glory, great things he hath done'? The pithy little choruses that I sang as a Christian teenager I still remember and love. Their carefully crafted words have made a deep impression.

Paul speaks here of singing 'to the Lord'. More surprising is his comment that we are also 'speaking to one another' as we sing. 'Praise, my soul, the king of heaven' is a mighty hymn of praise to God, but it is also exhorting and teaching the congregation about this wonderful God. 'Teach and admonish one another with all wisdom through psalms, hymns, and songs,' Paul says elsewhere (Colossians 3:16).

So the minister/organist/worship leader who chooses what we sing in church has a big teaching responsibility. And all those people who have been singing with us in all kinds of Christian settings down the years have been our teachers, singing great truths of the Christian faith into our hearts and lives. Let the people sing.

■ **PRAYER**
If you have a hymnbook at home, reading the words of a hymn can be a real tonic, and a great help to praying.

Romans 15:5–7 (NRSV)

Harmony with each other

May the God of steadfastness and encouragement grant you to live in harmony with one another, in accordance with Christ Jesus, so that together you may with one voice glorify the God and Father of our Lord Jesus Christ. Welcome one another, therefore, just as Christ has welcomed you, for the glory of God.

Visitors flock to a herbaceous border and admire the gorgeous fusion of colour. An endless variety of plants mass into a stunning summer attraction. Clashing colours and contrasting shapes harmonise into a work of art. Plants you think would not go together make room for each other and perfectly complement each other. Despite their many differences, the plants combine to support each other and produce a glorious overall impact.

Our passage is a prayer that church members in all their variety may do something similar: accept one another and live in harmony with one another to the glory of God. Jesus once said to his disciples, 'Be at peace with one another' (Mark 9:50). Then he went further. He made it possible for everyone to find their place in his church. May we share his attitude. There are many ways we can welcome people, introduce them, accompany them and generally help them to find their place in church life.

■ PRAYER

Pray that people of all backgrounds and ages will feel that they are accepted in church life and that they have a valued part to play, to the glory of God.

Galatians 5:13b; 6:2 (NRSV)

One another's burdens

Through love become slaves to one another... Bear one another's burdens, and in this way you will fulfil the law of Christ.

It was the end of the college year and I had to clear my digs. I packed cheerfully, not thinking that I had four substantial suitcases, in the days before luggage had wheels. It was a deserted Sunday morning. I slowly staggered halfway towards the nearby underground station, but then everything became too heavy. Clearly I would miss my train home. Just then, an older couple in a little car – were they on their way to church, I wonder? – drew up and offered to take me and my cases for the final stretch. I did not know them and never saw them again. But thanks to them, I caught my train.

Fulfilling the law of Christ is a lofty concept. But doing it is surprisingly down to earth: we do it by carrying one another's loads, according to the apostle Paul. What Christ is looking for is that we should make each other's lives easier, if we can. Lightening other people's loads is what servants used to do, and it is how he wants us to serve one another today.

People may be carrying burdens silently that we are unaware of. Let's take care we don't *add* to someone else's burden by a thoughtless word or action.

■ PRAYER

Lord Jesus, give me sensitivity and good sense to help people with what they are having to cope with. Amen

James 5:13–16 (NRSV, abridged)

Pray for one another

Are any among you suffering? They should pray... Are any among you sick?... The prayer of faith will save the sick... and anyone who has committed sins will be forgiven. Therefore confess your sins to one another, and pray for one another, so that you may be healed. The prayer of the righteous is powerful and effective.

Most churches have a slot on Sunday mornings when the congregation prays together for the wider church in the world. They also offer prayer for those who are sick or in particular need. Some churches have a regular prayer meeting to pray for the church. Church home groups often have a time when the members can pray for any needs they have. Sometimes supporters meet specially to pray for a particular mission partner overseas. Christian agencies publish a 'prayer diary' suggesting different needs day-by-day that supporters can pray for. It is a basic fact: Christians pray for one another.

Is 'sorry' the hardest word to say? What about the phrase 'that's all right': words of reconciliation and healing? Where Christians have wronged each other, they should confess it to each another, says our passage. Then they can pray with one another and for one another and share in the most powerful thing any of us can do.

■ PRAYER

If we say we will remember someone in our prayers, it is easy to forget. A slip of paper reminding us of those we mean to pray for can make sure it really happens.

1 John 4:10–12 (NIV)

Love one another

This is love: not that we loved God, but that he loved us and sent his Son as an atoning sacrifice for our sins. Dear friends, since God so loved us, we also ought to love one another. No one has ever seen God; but if we love one another, God lives in us and his love is made complete in us.

'What is love?' 'How can we see God?' They sound like children's questions. The answers given in these verses are practical and profound. God is the answer to the question about love, and love is the answer to the question about God.

Love in the Bible is very much a *doing* word. The greatest love in the world is what God *did* for us at the cross. But how can God be real if we can't see him? We see God living in his children as they love one another. Their love reveals God.

I think of a teenager who found herself living many miles away from her previous home after a traumatic and emotional time. She had no Christian background, but she came to flourish through the love, friendship and care of new friends and their church. In due course, she too came to believe, and she is now a much-respected children's worker and ordained minister. How to sum it up? Love won another.

■ **PRAYER**
Pray that Christians, worldwide and locally, may be known for their practical love, and so show God to the world.

Fruitful living

Tony Horsfall

Last year I celebrated my 70th birthday, a milestone in anyone's life. I felt God say to me that I still had one more adventure ahead of me, and I am up for the challenge. I hope you are too.

It is easy to feel in later life that our best days are behind us, but this is not true. We can still make a difference, whatever our age and wherever we are. The psalmist declared that the righteous 'will still bear fruit in old age, they will stay fresh and green' (Psalm 92:14, NIV). It is possible for us to flourish despite advancing years and, if we stay close to God, we can continue to be fruitful.

In these notes we look at the familiar passage in John 15:1–17 where Jesus speaks about the vine and the branches. I do not see any sell-by date here, nor any best-before limitation. The life it describes is for us all, whatever our stage in life. The promise is that if we abide in Christ, we will be fruitful.

John 15:16 (NIV)

The Father's purpose

'You did not choose me, but I chose you and appointed you so that you might go and bear fruit – fruit that will last – and so that whatever you ask in my name the Father will give you.'

Is a tomato a fruit or a vegetable? You will have your own opinion, but botanically it is classified as a fruit, while from a culinary perspective it is a vegetable.

There is no such confusion over grapes. They are definitely the fruit of the vine. The difficulty comes when we try to describe what Jesus had in mind when he speaks about spiritual fruit.

My definition is that fruit is 'the outward expression of the life of God within'. This kind of fruit is described in Galatians 5:22–23 as love, joy, peace, forbearance, kindness, goodness, faithfulness, gentleness and self-control. Any believer can produce this kind of fruit regardless of their age. Indeed, as we mature, we can display these Christlike qualities even more.

We can also say that we bear fruit when our actions display the compassionate love of Christ to others, 'bearing fruit in every good work' (Colossians 1:10). Again, age is no barrier when it comes to reflecting the love of God practically, even in small acts of kindness.

■ PRAYER

Lord, help me to be a person who bears much fruit, for this is still your purpose for my life. Amen

John 15:8; Matthew 7:19–20 (NIV)

The disciple's desire

'This is to my Father's glory, that you bear much fruit, showing yourselves to be my disciples... Every tree that does not bear good fruit is cut down and thrown into the fire. Thus, by their fruit you will recognise them.'

In our small garden, we have two apple trees and a cherry tree. Normally they each produce a good crop, but not this year. For some reason, only one of the trees was fruitful. At least I had some delicious eating apples.

The most common word used to describe believers in the New Testament is 'disciple'. As the word suggests, it means to be a disciplined follower of a master or teacher. When Simon Peter and the others decided to follow Jesus, it was with this in mind. They wanted to attach themselves to Jesus, learn from his teaching and become like him in their ways.

A distinguishing mark of true disciples is their desire to bear much fruit. They want to produce the fruit of the Spirit in their lives and demonstrate the love of God through their actions. In this way they prove the reality of their discipleship. They are recognised by their fruitfulness.

Not only does this please the Father but it also glorifies him. This is the ambition of every genuine disciple. Is it your desire?

■ **PRAYER**

Lord, help me to be a true disciple, bearing fruit in all I do and say. Amen

John 15:4–5 (NIV)

The vine and the branches

'Remain in me, as I also remain in you. No branch can bear fruit by itself; it must remain in the vine. Neither can you bear fruit unless you remain in me. I am the vine; you are the branches. If you remain in me and I in you, you will bear much fruit; apart from me you can do nothing.'

I wonder if you love words. I do, which is why I am a writer. I love to play around with words, to savour their sound and meaning. Choosing just the right word is important to me, which is why I regret the choice of words here in the NIV translation. Instead of the word 'remain', I much prefer the word 'abide', which is used in older versions.

To abide means to make our home somewhere, to establish a dwelling place. Using the illustration of the way a branch abides in the vine, Jesus promises that he will come to reside within us and share his life with us. He also promises that if we abide in him, we will bear much fruit. It will happen naturally and easily.

We abide in Christ as we worship, pray, read the scriptures and share fellowship with others. These practices bring us close to God and allow his life to flow through us. When this happens, we bear fruit without even realising it.

■ **PRAYER**

Lord, help me to live in you, as you live in me. Amen

John 15:1–3 (NIV)

Pruning

'I am the true vine, and my Father is the gardener. He cuts off every branch in me that bears no fruit, while every branch that does bear fruit he prunes so that it will be even more fruitful. You are already clean because of the word I have spoken to you.'

Most gardeners know that the secret to fruitfulness is regular pruning. Fruit trees need to be well cared for and tended regularly. This is especially true of the vine, which left alone will easily grow out of control.

Pruning is the act of removing that which is dead or diseased, and cutting off any excess growth that may spoil the quality of the fruit which is forming on the vine. It seems a very drastic action, but it is essential if there is to be a good crop of grapes.

One way in which God prunes us is by convicting us of our sin. His Spirit stirs our conscience to tell us when we are doing anything that is displeasing to God and unhelpful to our witness for him. It is important that we listen to this still, small voice and cooperate with the work of God in our hearts, letting go of anything that might hinder our walk with him. He speaks only to build us up, never to tear us down.

■ **PRAYER**

Lord, help me to be responsive to the conviction of your Spirit. Amen

John 15:6; Acts 2:42 (NIV)

Detached?

'**If you do not remain in me, you are like a branch that is thrown away and withers; such branches are picked up, thrown into the fire and burned...**' **They devoted themselves to the apostles' teaching and to fellowship, to the breaking of bread and to prayer.**

I went walking recently with a friend through woods near his home. He has a log burner in his house and he often collects branches that have been broken off to take back with him. Once dried, they make excellent fuel for the stove.

Jesus warns us here that if we allow ourselves to become detached from him, we will eventually dry up spiritually and become unfruitful. He is not saying that we will be punished or cast aside. That is to take the illustration too far. He is reminding us that if we cease to depend on him, we will no longer be able to bear fruit. We may lose our joy and our peace.

What might cause us to wither? It happens when we neglect going to church, or reading the Bible, or praying and so on. Sometimes it happens inadvertently because we are unwell or housebound. Whatever the reason, it is easily remedied. We can quickly reconnect with God when we return to our normal spiritual patterns.

■ **PRAYER**

Lord, show me how to stay connected to you in the midst of my particular circumstances. I don't want to wither. Amen

John 15:7; 1 John 5:14 (NIV)

Asking

'If you remain in me and my words remain in you, ask whatever you wish, and it will be done for you...' This is the confidence we have in approaching God: that if we ask anything according to his will, he hears us.

My two grandsons often come to stay with me, and we have a lot of fun. They always seem to be hungry and pester me for something to eat, especially sweets. They ask so nicely, and their asking melts my heart. I usually give way.

Disciples of Jesus, whatever their age, love to ask their heavenly Father for good things. That is the essence of prayer, and it is a wonderful privilege to be able to approach him with our requests. But how do we know what to pray for?

Jesus reminds us that our asking should come from our reading of his word, for the Bible reveals to us the will of God. We are not to ask selfishly, but rather ask in line with his will. This is the best way to make sure our prayers are answered.

The more we allow God's word to dwell in us richly (Colossians 3:16), the easier it becomes to discern his will. And one thing the Father wants is that we bear much fruit. We can ask for this with the persistence of a little child.

■ **PRAYER**

Lord, today I ask that you make me fruitful in every way. Amen

John 15:9; 1 John 4:10 (NIV)

Receiving

'As the Father has loved me, so have I loved you. Now remain in my love…' This is love: not that we loved God, but that he loved us and sent his Son as an atoning sacrifice for our sins.

A friend was devastated when her fiancé broke off their engagement. 'Who will love me now?' she cried, feelings of rejection and unworthiness swirling around inside her. Only when she turned to God, and received again his unconditional love for her, did she find peace and the strength to begin again.

The first fruit of the Spirit is love. Indeed, we could say that every other fruit is in fact a manifestation of love. Therefore, to be fruitful we need to be full of love. However, human love will never be enough. We must receive – and keep on receiving – the limitless love of God into our hearts.

Jesus demonstrated real love when he laid down his life for us on the cross. The Spirit wants to pour that same love into our hearts to remind us that we are his beloved children, but also to enable us to love others.

If you want to live a fruitful life, ask God to fill you afresh with heavenly love each day. Then you will be able to love others in your words and actions.

■ **PRAYER**

Lord, make me a more loving person. Fill me with Calvary love as I wait before you. Amen

John 15:10–11 (NIV)

Obeying

'If you keep my commands, you will remain in my love, just as I have kept my Father's commands and remain in his love. I have told you this so that my joy may be in you and that your joy may be complete.'

Early on in the pandemic, we were encouraged to wear face masks. This was not easy at first, and many people found it difficult to comply, but it was for our own sake and also the well-being of others. Yet some rebelled. 'No one tells me what to do,' was their attitude.

As sinful human beings, we do not find obedience easy. Like Adam and Eve in the garden, we want to rebel against the commands of God, but they are given for our good. They express his wisdom and care for us and are in no way a burden or imposition.

When we obey our heavenly Father, and gladly accept his will for our life, we find his love flowing more fully into our hearts. Not only that, but his joy wells up within us. Thus the life of obedience is a life of love and joy – in other words, a fruitful life that blesses others too.

As you read the Bible, listen to what God has to say to you and be sure to act upon anything the Spirit asks you to do. This is the way of blessing.

■ **PRAYER**

Speak, Lord, your servant is listening. Amen

John 15:12–14, 17 (NIV)

Loving

'My command is this: love each other as I have loved you. Greater love has no one than this: to lay down one's life for one's friends. You are my friends if you do what I command... This is my command: love each other.'

In the village where I grew up there is a war memorial with the names of those men who died during the two World Wars. Many of the families who lost loved ones still live in the village. The inscription also includes part of today's reading – 'Greater love has no man than this: to lay down his life for his friends.'

The greatest example of love was the sacrificial death of Jesus on the cross, dying to save a sinful world. We are the beneficiaries of such matchless love and are called upon as our response to love others.

The Christian life was never intended to be a private affair. It is meant to be lived in community with others, but such a community only works if those involved have learned to love each other sacrificially. Then, as the life of the community deepens with the giving and receiving of love, it can become a place of welcome and acceptance for others. This is God's blueprint for the church, and we bear fruit when we involve ourselves as much as we are able.

■ **PRAYER**

Lord, thank you for placing me within your family, the church. Amen

John 15:15; 10:27 (NIV)

Knowing

'I no longer call you servants, because a servant does not know his master's business. Instead, I have called you friends, for everything that I learned from my Father I have made known to you... My sheep listen to my voice: I know them and they follow me.'

Do you remember the British Telecom adverts in the 1990s that had the strapline, 'It's good to talk'? This marketing strategy was immensely successful and was based around encouraging people to talk more together on the telephone, sharing what the experts called 'reciprocated confidences'.

A mark of close friendship is this willingness to share deeply. Jesus says that he wants his disciples to be more than servants, dutifully obeying him. Rather, he sees them as his friends, and he desires to share his heart and mind with them. This is a wonderful invitation to intimacy with Jesus, to fellowship of the highest order.

As we learn to abide in Christ, we will find that we begin to move from being servants into becoming his friends. We will develop a clearer understanding of what he wants us to do and a growing ability to hear his voice directing us. In this way our lives will be even more fruitful and our discipleship more real. We will be about the Father's business. How do you see yourself – servant or friend?

■ **PRAYER**

Lord, I welcome your invitation to a deeper friendship. What a privilege! Amen

The Gift of Years

Debbie Thrower is the pioneer of BRF's Anna Chaplaincy for Older People ministry, offering spiritual care to older people, and is widely involved in training and advocacy.

Visit **annachaplaincy.org.uk** to find out more.

Debbie writes...

Jesus' stories helped describe the kingdom of God, the reign of God, in our extraordinary, fallen world. We all need stories to make sense of life. From our earliest childhood there's the delight of being read to, of discovering adventure stories, of imagining heroes and villains.

It is extraordinary to think how Jesus learnt from his mother Mary – was taught to pray (as many of us were by our mothers and fathers), to commit words of scripture to memory so they might comfort him in times of trial. The Word was taught the value of words by a humble young woman whose intellect he would outgrow, moving so far beyond her understanding as to cause perplexity and sorrow, but never out of reach of her love.

As *we* grow older, we come to rely on the stories of our lives to weave a narrative that is our own, unique to us, with all its pleasures and pain. This issue's skilful writers help us reflect on our own life stories, comparing and contrasting the glimpses of other people's lives with the circumstances of our own life story until the point, perhaps, when words become superfluous?

Jesus' story is the paradigm for our own lives on earth. Enjoy the insights in these pages into Christ the king, Christ the healer, pointing the way to lives of quiet fruitfulness.

Best wishes

Debbie

Meet Andrew Rudd

Andrew Rudd is a Cheshire-based teacher and poet. He was Cheshire Poet Laureate in 2006 and is currently poet-in-residence at Manchester Cathedral, with a PhD in poetry and spirituality. He is involved in training ordinands and lay workers in spirituality and is a spiritual director and lay reader. He is inching towards retirement by doing less and less paid work and finding more time to 'play' in the widest sense of the word. Married to Wendy, they have two grandchildren. Isla, big sister to Ollie, was two when she inspired the poem which follows this interview. Andrew was brought up in the Plymouth Brethren but was gradually drawn to a wider faith after he left home for university. He takes up the story some years later:

I was 50 when there was a cash crisis in the educational advisory service in Cheshire and I took what I hesitate to call 'early retirement'. But I stopped what I was doing and began working part-time doing teacher training at Manchester Metropolitan University. That gave me time to do other things, including a Master's in creative writing with Carol Ann Duffy and Simon Armitage. That's when I really got going with poetry.

What's the link between writing and spirituality?

To me, writing is a very important place of spiritual discovery. Writing is about finding things out that you didn't know when you picked up your pen. It's not that you have an idea and put it down on paper – the paper is the place where it happens. That's what my PhD was about: constructing spirituality through writing.

For Andrew, as for many people, the long periods of lockdown during the pandemic impacted his creativity:

Some people wrote reams and reams because of the pandemic, but I actually dried up a lot. It just wasn't a good time for writing – or reading for that matter.

But there was another kind of writing which I did during lockdown, which was when I was out walking, talking into my phone and then transcribing it when I came back. If I wrote any poetry over that time – though it was a very lean time for writing poetry – it came out of that walking and talking.

Andrew and Wendy also spent a lot of time making audio church services on CD:

We made 30 copies every week for people in the church who didn't have access to the technology for online services. The demographic was often people over 80, who were very isolated through the pandemic. So that was a case of acquiring a whole new set of skills, essentially in making radio programmes: recording and editing. I think that was a major zone of my creativity during the pandemic.

What is 'the gift of years' for Andrew?

I suppose… it's a gift and a curse really. Where I'm sitting now, I'm looking at my poetry collection, which is a *lot* of books, and they fill me with joy because they're poetry. But they also fill me with a deep sense of foreboding, because I know I can't read them all. And that's representative of so much else: there isn't time in my life to do all that I might want to do. That's the conundrum of living with this lovely residue of years, but also learning to live with joy and delight in the moment. That to me is the issue of the second half of life and its spirituality: what do I do with this conundrum?

And is it really the gift of years, because I find it in the very small child: the capacity to value the things that are beautiful and are transient, and their not lasting is what makes them beautiful. If you could capture them, they would no longer be beautiful. It's finding that delight and freshness, and that newness at this time of life. Sometimes I do, and my aspiration is to live more and more in that space.

I think every poem is an attempt – not to capture it, that's the wrong word, that's like the pressed flower – but to maybe hold it, like Isla in this poem, to hold it in the hand, the thing which is so insignificant, but which turns out to be God. That's what a poem tries to do, to be a little container for something of that, for a little while. It's not possible but it's always worth trying.

Tell us how your poem, 'Isla and Baby Jesus', came about.

We got our nativity set from Oxfam Trading years and years ago – a very simple wooden set – and we still have a Christmas ritual of putting it out with the grandchildren and talking through the Christmas story. This was the first time for Isla. We talked about the baby Jesus, which is just a little tiny wooden peg, barely a centimetre long, and we carefully gave it to her to put into the manger. She held it with this wonderful gesture, cupping it so carefully in her hands, which was so eucharistic. The poem is simply the observation of that moment... and the deep thrill of it.

Isla and Baby Jesus

you were only two and you didn't know
the little wooden peg you held

that you lifted so carefully out of the little manger
in the nativity set was God

but you held God with such gentleness
and showed God all the trees and you bent low

to your hands so that you could nearly
touch God's face and then placed

God in the manger of my hands
the cradle of my fingers

like a wafer like a promise
like grace

Andrew Rudd, used with kind permission

At Home in Advent – Gordon Giles

Rochester Diocese has been a key partner with Anna Chaplaincy since the early days of the ministry, so when popular BRF author Gordon Giles became canon chancellor at Rochester Cathedral in the autumn of 2020, it was natural for him to extend a welcoming hand when Debbie Thrower and members of her husband's cycling club happened to be riding by. The group was given a special tour of the cathedral by Christine Bostock, cathedral guide and Anna Chaplain. Here's an extract from Gordon's popular *At Home in Advent: A domestic journey from Advent to Epiphany*, BRF's Advent book for 2020.

Welcome aboard! Welcome to an Advent journey that goes nowhere but takes us everywhere, and through it all, stays at home!…

Do you remember the *Blue Peter* Advent crown? Every year the long-running children's programme used to show the nation's children how to make an Advent crown, a decoration for the season, fashioned out of coat hangers and tinsel. The candle holders were made out of bottle tops and the tinsel wrapped around it. It was simple, but not a little dangerous: fireproof tinsel was less readily available in the 1970s, when John Noakes and his successors did this. The *Blue Peter* Advent crown was a national phenomenon in much the same way that Advent calendars containing chocolate (or other treats) are today.

Many churches have Advent wreaths, adorned with greenery and high-quality candles. Church Advent candles generally consist of three purple, one pink and one white. Different traditions account for these coloured candles in different ways, associating them with different themes for each Sunday. These four candles tell a story, before we reach the fifth one, the white one, which is for Jesus, lit at Christmas.

Christingle candles also appear at this time of year. This relatively modern tradition gives us an orange, representing the world; a candle, representing Christ as the light of the world; a red ribbon wrapped around the orange, representing the blood of Christ; and dried fruits or sweets on cocktail sticks pushed into the orange, representing the fruits of the earth and the four seasons, or perhaps the wounds of Christ. Suffering and light are thereby connected.

The white candle of church Advent tradition unites and makes sense of all of our candle-lighting traditions, whatever colour they may be. For whether the candles we light are representative of biblical people, characters in the nativity story or symbols of prayer for the sick and dying or deceased, ultimately and universally, all is light.

When we light a candle, we create, share and acknowledge a little bit of light. It is fragile light, a 'little light of mine' that shines in the darkness, to add to all the other lights and to join with the overwhelming greater light of Christ. Our little light, whether lit at home or in church, represents the light of Christ, which itself reminds us of two vital aspects of our faith: Christ, born at Bethlehem to bring light into the world, to save us, to be a beacon of hope shining in this dark world of sin; and Christ, the Easter light, who, although he was born into a dark world, concluded his walk on this sad, blue planet in a blaze of resurrection light. So every Advent candle is an Easter candle too, and every Easter candle a reminder of the Advent hope, which will yet emerge as resurrection light.

The other aspect of any candle, especially in Advent, is that it is also a metaphor for life and death. The candle is a *memento mori*, a reminder of mortality. Candles die – their wick burns down and the flame is extinguished. Every candle is an Advent candle, because it points us towards those four last things.

There is no escaping this: being born, we will die, and this is a theme for reflection in Advent as we draw nearer to that time when our ultimate salvation inevitably comes (see Romans 13:11–14). Yet the candles have been lit to symbolise, even be part of, that greater light, and so the dying candle points us not only to our death, but also by its very incandescence to the resurrection light beyond. When our little light goes out, we begin another journey to a greater light.

The poet and preacher John Donne (1572–1631) put this beautifully in a passage in a sermon which is now often used as a prayer, especially at funerals. He speaks of 'No darkness, nor dazzling', that is, no candles and no need for candles. There are no hopes nor fears, that is, nothing to worry about and therefore nothing to hope for either; there is no need for hope when perfect love has cast out fear. The place where that will happen, where it *has* happened, is the place of equal eternity in the presence of God.

You can order a copy of *At Home in Advent* from page 62.

God is king

Ro Willoughby

I wonder what you think about when you hear the word 'king'? You may have childhood memories of kings and queens sitting on a grand throne in a fairy-tale castle. Or you may think of kings in the Old Testament – Saul, David, Solomon, Ahab, Josiah – the good and the not-so-good. It may be kings from school history lessons such as William the Conqueror, Louis XIV, Henry VIII, Edward VIII. You might think of a chess piece or an academic school or college. But you probably will not have immediately thought of God as king.

Yet the idea of God's kingship runs throughout the Bible. This is the theme of these Bible reflections. God rules the world as king. He longed to be king of his chosen people. Wise men came in search of the baby king in a humble home. When Christ came to this earth, the kingdom of God came near. Jesus rode into Jerusalem on a donkey and the crowds cheered him on as their king.

Christians now live as children of God's kingdom and expect Christ to return to this earth as king. For this reason, the Christian calendar places the Feast of Christ the King on the Sunday before Advent. Jesus the king was born in an unannounced way the first time. The second time Jesus will come as king of the whole world.

My hope is that in this series you will be led to a deeper appreciation and worship of God as king.

1 Samuel 8:6–9, 18–22 (NIV, abridged)

We want a king!

When [the people] said, 'Give us a king to lead us,' this displeased Samuel, so he prayed to the Lord and the Lord told him: 'Listen to all that the people are saying to you... Warn them solemnly... You will cry out for relief from the king you have chosen, but the Lord will not answer you in that day'... 'No!' [the people] said. 'We want a king over us. Then we shall be like all the other nations...' The Lord answered, 'Listen to them and give them a king.'

Richard the Lionheart was king of England from 1189 to 1199. He only ever spent a few months in England. Instead, he led the Third Crusade to the holy land and conducted wars in his lands in France. He is what we'd call a bad king who neglected his kingdom.

God's people wanted a king like that, now they'd settled in the promised land – a king to fight in battle. God himself wasn't that sort of king. Samuel asked God for wisdom. He told them a king would claim their land, flocks and children. But they continued their demand. So God agreed.

We may want our lives to be different. We may envy someone. We may want change. The first thing Samuel did was to talk with God. That's very wise, for the more we talk with God, the more able we will be to discern God's way. Our trust in him will deepen. The people of Israel settled for the second best. It brought them endless trouble.

■ **PRAYER**

What makes you discontented or envious? Tell God about it and remember he can be trusted.

2 Samuel 23:1–4 (NIV, abridged)

A man after my own heart

The last words of David... 'The Spirit of the Lord spoke through me; his word was on my tongue. The God of Israel spoke, the Rock of Israel said to me: "When one rules over people in righteousness, when he rules in the fear of God, he is like the light of morning at sunrise on a cloudless morning."'

We can look back on our lives and see only our failures. King David could certainly do that. He was a fierce warrior king who made many enemies and many mistakes. Nonetheless, he is known as a man after God's own heart. In his last words, we see he recognises God as the real king ruling through David.

Here are four things David did that explain why God loved him so much. As a young man, he courageously fought Goliath the giant, coming 'in the name of the Lord Almighty', completely dependent upon God. King Saul hunted David down to kill him. But David refused to kill Saul, because Saul was God's anointed king. When David realised he'd committed murder and adultery, he declared that he had sinned against God alone. He wrote many psalms declaring his love for and trust in God.

■ **PRAYER**

This gives us hope. We've all had successes and failures. But what really matters is that we have known God's love for us and have loved him. Think of times when you've experienced God's love, then declare your love for him in return.

Psalm 95:3–5; Psalm 97:1–2 (NIV, abridged)

God is king

For the Lord is the great God, the great King above all gods. In his hand are the depths of the earth, and the mountain peaks belong to him. The sea is his, for he made it... The Lord reigns... righteousness and justice are the foundation of his throne.

In the early months of 2020, a new virus swept around the world. Covid-19 rapidly threatened lives and the world economy in an unprecedented way. People felt afraid and uncertain. As Christians, it is vitally important that we hold fast to the truth that the Lord is king over the whole world.

The psalms often focus on God as king. Just as he brought order out of chaos when he created the earth, so God can bring order and peace. He is the great, all-powerful king, greater than any other god (not that there is any other). He is good and truthful. He is just and fair. He sits upon a throne to hear the requests of those who come before him. Chaos may seem to be all around, but nothing takes God by surprise. He is powerfully with us in all the troubles of our world.

■ **PRAYER**

Repeat the words of this 19th-century hymn as you reflect on the brokenness across the globe: 'The Lord is king! Lift up your voice, O earth, and all you heavens, rejoice; from world to world the song shall ring: the Lord omnipotent is king!'*

* 'The Lord is King!', Josiah Conder (1789–1855)

Jeremiah 23:1, 3–6 (NIV, abridged)

A shepherd-king comes

'Woe to the shepherds who are destroying and scattering the sheep of my pasture!' declares the Lord... 'I myself will gather the remnant of my flock... and will bring them back to their pasture... I will place shepherds over them who will tend them... The days are coming,' declares the Lord, 'when I will raise up for David... a King who will reign wisely and do what is just and right.'

I sometimes listen to the early morning radio programme *Farming today*. In the late winter/early spring it often includes interviews on the lambing season. Farmers work hard, 24 hours a day, but they always speak of wanting the best for their ewes and newborn lambs. They are good shepherds.

The kings of Israel are sometimes referred to as shepherds, most notably King David. Yet many of them were worthless shepherds who cared neither for God nor his people. The prophet Jeremiah brought God's word to these kings. He tells them that another king, another shepherd, is coming, a descendant of King David who will be just, behave rightly – a good shepherd.

Recently, as a friend was dying in a hospital in the Middle East, her parents read John 10 to her via a video link. They were entrusting her into the arms of the good shepherd. He held her as a little lamb in his arms. He holds each one of us and keeps us safe.

■ **PRAYER**

Jesus, the good shepherd who gave his life for his sheep, hold me safe today in your arms. Amen

Matthew 2:1–2, 9–11 (NIV, abridged)

A baby king

Magi from the east came to Jerusalem and asked, 'Where is the one who has been born king of the Jews? We saw his star when it rose and have come to worship him'... They went on their way... The star they had seen... went ahead of them until it stopped over the place where the child... They bowed down and worshipped him. Then they opened their treasures and presented him with gifts of gold, frankincense and myrrh.

Most parents look at their newborn baby and wonder what will become of their child. They cannot know if their dreams will become reality. But Mary knew her son's destiny, although its significance at that point was beyond her grasp. The Magi's visit would have assured her that hers was no ordinary son. They had travelled so far to see him; they worshipped him; they lavished gifts upon him.

Here are three types of king: 1) These travellers, popularly called 'kings', not wise men, came searching for the true king. 2) Wicked King Herod, hearing about this baby king, ordered baby boys to be slaughtered. 3) The child Jesus, growing up in a normal family in an obscure part of the world, was God in human form, one like us, a king in the making.

■ **PRAYER**

'As they offered gifts most rare, at that cradle rude and bare; so may we with holy joy, pure and free from sin's alloy, all our costliest treasures bring, Christ to thee, our heavenly King.'* Amen

* 'As with gladness, men of old', W. Chatterton Dix (1837–98)

John 6:11, 14–15 (NIV)

We must make Jesus king!

Jesus then took the loaves, gave thanks, and distributed to those who were seated as much as they wanted. He did the same with the fish... After the people saw the sign Jesus performed, they began to say, 'Surely this is the Prophet who is to come into the world.' Jesus, knowing they intended to come and make him king by force, withdrew again to a mountain by himself.

In the early days of the coronavirus pandemic in 2020, many supermarket shelves were stripped bare. People wondered, often for the first time, 'Is there going to be enough food for me to feed my family?'

The story in today's verses must be one of the best-known in the gospel – Jesus feeding over 5,000 people, a miracle which left thousands of people happily satisfied. He did it with minimum fuss. The crowds may not have thought much about the identity of Jesus, this attention-grabbing teacher they had come to listen to. But once he'd fed them, they certainly wondered who he was. He must be the Prophet. He could provide for their basic human needs. They just had to make him their king.

But Jesus was having none of it. He simply absented himself. He wasn't that sort of king. He came to provide for more than just basic bodily needs; he'd come to meet people's fundamental spiritual need to be put right with God.

■ PRAYER

Jesus calls us to trust him to provide for all our needs, physically and spiritually. King Jesus, help me to trust you to provide for me in every way. Amen

Matthew 13:45–46 (NIV)

The kingdom of heaven

'The kingdom of heaven is like a merchant looking for fine pearls. When he found one of great value, he went away and sold everything he had and bought it.'

I enjoy telling a group of children a version of this parable of Jesus. I tip out my collection of scarves made of mixed materials, some old and frayed, ordinary patterns and colours, various shapes and sizes. The children are mildly interested. Then I unwrap my Kashmiri silk scarf. It feels soft and delicate. It's a riot of deep glittering blues, purples and emeralds, shot with threads of silver. It is huge. The children crowd round to stroke it between their fingers. They would swap all my other scarves for this one.

That's what this merchant did: sold everything for the pearl he valued more than anything else. It was a drastic decision, presumably with serious consequences.

Jesus did just that. He came to establish his kingdom on earth, a kingdom governed by God's values, a kingdom focused on worshipping and serving the king. To do this, he exchanged the glory of heaven and took on our humanity. He made himself 'of no reputation'. He showed how to live in his kingdom. In the end, he gave everything by dying on the cross. What a king!

■ **PRAYER**

In the Lord's Prayer, we acknowledge God's kingdom. Slowly pray this today, reflecting on what it means to say, 'Your kingdom come, your will be done on earth as in heaven.'

John 12:12–14a (NIV)

Long live the king!

The next day the great crowd that had come for the festival heard that Jesus was on his way to Jerusalem. They took palm branches and went out to meet him, shouting, 'Hosanna!' 'Blessed is he who comes in the name of the Lord!' 'Blessed is the king of Israel!' Jesus found a young donkey and sat upon it.

Guests at a church wedding wait for the moment when the bride begins her walk down the aisle. All chatter ceases. Everyone stands up. Most strain to catch a glimpse of her. She's arrived.

Crowds wanted to catch a glimpse of Jesus as he rode on the donkey into Jerusalem. They'd heard about him. This day he was riding on a donkey, as King Solomon did on his way to his coronation. Could this be the long-promised Messiah, come to rescue them from the Romans?

But King Jesus was not that sort of king. He was a king who would suffer for his people. He was a king who could fight in battle but chose not to. It was not in God's plan. He would die to free all people from the burden of their sin, to make it possible for them to have a never-ending relationship with God, his Father.

■ **PRAYER**

We sing, 'Make way, make way for Christ the king!' Jesus Christ, help me to make way for you in my life today. Thank you that I'm forgiven and freed from the burden of my sin. Amen

John 19:19–22 (NIV)

King of the Jews

Pilate had a notice... fastened to the cross. It read: 'Jesus of Nazareth, the king of the Jews.' Many of the Jews read this sign... written in Aramaic, Latin and Greek. The chief priests of the Jews protested to Pilate, 'Do not write "The King of the Jews", but that this man claimed to be king of the Jews.' Pilate answered, 'What I have written, I have written.'

Has anyone has ever told you how attractive or brilliant you are, when they really mean the complete opposite? Mocking sarcasm is horribly destructive.

Governor Pontius Pilate served the Roman Emperor. For him there was no other king, certainly not Jesus. He may have wanted to humiliate Jesus by calling him king, but Pilate's main aim was to belittle the Jewish authorities. 'This defenceless carpenter from Nazareth is the best you can conjure up for a king!'

The Jewish authorities didn't believe Jesus was a king either. They expected someone far more powerful and on their side. They sarcastically mocked Jesus' claims.

Jesus' cross and crown of thorns were more than instruments of torture. Here was Jesus' throne on which he was crowned. He didn't die just for the Jews but also for Gentiles from across that part of the world who could read Jesus' title 'King of the Jews', in three languages. On the cross Jesus spread out his arms to welcome all to become part of God's kingdom.

■ **PRAYER**

Open your arms wide as you imagine King Jesus welcoming you into his kingdom, and be thankful.

Revelation 21:3–5 (NIV, abridged)

The king returns

I heard a loud voice from the throne saying, 'Look! God's dwelling-place is now among the people, and he will dwell with them... He will wipe every tear from their eyes. There will be no more death or mourning or crying or pain...' He who was seated on the throne said, 'I am making everything new!'

The coronavirus pandemic has made me so conscious of the fragility of our world. Fear, uncertainty and sorrow all around us. The health of the globe, along with economic and social structures, all endangered.

There have always been many reasons for us to be sad, to fear or to struggle. But Christians know that Jesus will return to this earth, not this time as a baby but as a king. There will be a new heaven and a new earth. Everything will be made new – no more death, mourning, crying or pain. Jesus the king will sit upon his throne to reign over his kingdom. We will dwell with him.

As we look forward to the day of Christ's return, we can find courage in the challenges of the present. Today, may God grant us his comfort and reassurance in our hope that all things will be made new.

■ **PRAYER**

A six-year-old once told me that if God came to stay forever in her house, she'd give him some slippers. There'd be no sadness nor tears. Can you imagine that? Give thanks that Christ is coming to reign.

Christ, our healer
Angela Tilby

Although the Bible is composed of many different books written over thousands of years, Christians have always believed that it tells one story, the story of our salvation. This story begins in the garden of Eden and ends in the heavenly city. It is the story of all humanity, and it is also the story of each one of us. When we read scripture, we are reading messages from God, a commentary on our lives.

The Advent season is one of expectation. We are looking forward to the coming of Christ and recognising our need of God's healing love. As we journey through life, we often become more aware of the mistakes we have made and the wrongs we have done. This can be a chastening experience, but it can also be a liberating one. Human brokenness is like sickness. When we know the diagnosis, there is a good chance that we can be healed. These readings have been chosen to help us focus on God's promise of salvation, a promise made to each one of us, a promise which God is fulfilling even as we wait for him.

Genesis 3:8–10 (NRSV)

God seeks Adam

[Adam and Eve] heard the sound of the Lord God walking in the garden at the time of the evening breeze, and the man and his wife hid themselves from the presence of the Lord God among the trees of the garden. But the Lord God called to the man, and said to him, 'Where are you?' He said, 'I heard the sound of you in the garden, and I was afraid, because I was naked; and I hid myself.'

To be human is to be vulnerable, and as we get older we often become more aware of just how vulnerable we are. It is natural to try to compensate for this, but there is no shame in simply being ourselves in God's presence.

God says to Adam 'Where are you?', not because God doesn't know, but because Adam is ashamed. He has good reason for his shame, but often our shame is about things we cannot help. God already knows us as we are and as we shall be in Christ. When he says, 'Where are you?', it is because he wants to share his divine life with us. Seek him today and let him find you, just as you are. Let him refresh your soul with the breeze of his Spirit.

■ **PRAYER**

Here I am, Lord, in your presence, ready to receive your love, ready to do your will. Help me to put my trust in you and to know you as my Saviour and my God. Amen

Psalm 139:13–14 (NRSV)

Fearfully and wonderfully made

For it was you who formed my inward parts; you knit me together in my mother's womb. I praise you, for I am fearfully and wonderfully made. Wonderful are your works; that I know very well.

We live in a world which is marvellously interconnected – from sub-atomic particles to galaxies, from micro-organisms to elephants and whales. The human brain is itself a universe of connectivity. Though we are grounded in the earthiness of existence, we also reach beyond ourselves, seeking fulfilment both in this life and beyond it.

God has made us of the earth but has put eternity in our hearts. And God does not stand apart from us, but comes to seek us in Christ, his beloved Son. He calls us by name and guides us day by day, if we will let him. Jesus spoke of God knowing the sparrows. How much more he knows us.

Remembering God's all-encompassing presence helps us to live gracefully in the present moment, not regretting our past, nor fearing our future, but having 'an attitude of gratitude', counting our blessings.

■ **PRAYER**

Lord God, all existence is a miracle, a work of art. Help me to see your loving and intricate work in the human body and mind, and to trust you, night and day, so that, whatever happens in me and around me, I may rest in your wondrous love. Amen

Isaiah 40:6–8 (NRSV)

The word of our God

A voice says, 'Cry out!' And I said, 'What shall I cry?' All people are grass, their constancy is like the flower of the field. The grass withers, the flower fades, when the breath of the Lord blows upon it; surely the people are grass. The grass withers, the flower fades; but the word of our God shall stand forever.

Isaiah was one of the greatest of the Old Testament prophets, and yet he had his moments of doubt and uncertainty. Here, he hears the voice of God calling him to cry out to his people, yet he does not know what his message should be. As he looks around him, he can see only human frailty.

People are not reliable. They get things wrong, they fail and, like all living things, they wither, fade and die. There is no such thing as permanence on earth. Yet this is not the end of the story. God's word is his very being. He has spoken us into life, and that life-giving word is never silenced or contradicted. Isaiah is the prophet of the incarnation: he looks forward to the coming of the Messiah who will restore all things. God's word can be trusted.

■ PRAYER

Lord God, when I have nothing to say and when I feel I have nothing to give, keep me trusting in your word, for your speech is my salvation: Christ, within, the hope of glory. Amen

Isaiah 64:7–8 (NRSV)

The hidden face

There is no one who calls on your name, or attempts to take hold of you; for you have hidden your face from us, and have delivered us into the hand of our iniquity. Yet, O Lord, you are our Father; we are the clay, and you are our potter; we are all the work of your hand.

Our Christian forebears felt that they lived in some sense before God's face. Everything that they did and thought was known to him. But today we live in a society that has lost much of its sense of God. Patterns of belief which once bound us together have fragmented, and we can no longer call on a common morality or sense of purpose.

It is not surprising that we see elements of corruption and deceit in public life. There are constant temptations to put me and my interests first. As a society, we reap what we sow. This is what the prophet means when he says we are in 'the hand of our iniquity'. Yet, the prophet also reminds us that we are closer to God than we think. Even as we fret about the state of the world, God is moulding our lives, our characters, our choices and our future.

■ **PRAYER**

Lord, shape me and mould me to be what you would have me be.
Help me to trust your workmanship and to know that, even when your face is hidden, I am safe in your hands. Amen

Psalm 119:145–148 (NRSV)

In the watches of the night

With my whole heart I cry; answer me, O Lord. I will keep your statutes. I cry to you; save me, that I may observe your decrees. I rise before dawn and call for help; I put my hope in your words. My eyes are awake before each watch of the night, that I may meditate on your promise.

It is an ancient tradition to believe that when we pray with the psalms, we pray with Christ. This goes back to the gospels, where Christ often quotes from the psalms, especially when he is explaining why he has to die and that he will rise again.

Here, in this psalm, we can imagine Christ taking on the prayers of those who are awake though the night. We can think of him in the desolation of Gethsemane, or getting up before dawn to pray as he so often did.

Christ's prayer at night is imitated by monks and nuns, who often get up for a 'night office' while the rest of the world is sleeping. They gather up the unspoken prayers of those who watch through the night to protect others, and those for whom sleep is difficult.

■ PRAYER

Lord, the darkness is not dark to you. You know the troubles of my heart, my hopes and my longings. Keep me close to you in the lonely and silent hours, in the restless hours, in the hours of sleep and when I wake. Amen

Isaiah 35:3–4 (NRSV)

Here is your God

Strengthen the weak hands, and make firm the feeble knees. Say to those that are of fearful heart, 'Be strong, do not fear! Here is your God. He will come with vengeance, with terrible recompense. He will come and save you.'

One of our deepest human instincts is a sense of fairness. Even very young children are quick to complain, 'It's not fair.'

The God we seek in our prayers, the God revealed in Jesus Christ, is a God of justice. He does not side with the strong against the weak, or value the rich more than the poor. He is *always* with those who are oppressed, rejected, impoverished or neglected.

It is easy to despair today that money has become the measure of everything and that social status seems to depend entirely on wealth. Yet God rejects this false sense of values. When he comes to us in Christ, he comes to set things right, to shock the self-satisfied out of their complacency and to make the fragile strong in his strength. Above all, he gives us hope. However worthless life has made us feel, we are of infinite worth to him.

■ PRAYER

Holy God, holy and strong, holy and immortal, have mercy on us. Strengthen us in our weakness, set us free by your mighty power and send us your everlasting mercy in Jesus Christ, our Lord. Amen

Malachi 4:2–3 (NRSV)

The sun of righteousness

But for you who revere my name the sun of righteousness shall rise, with healing in its wings. You shall go out leaping like calves from the stall. And you shall tread down the wicked, for they will be ashes under the soles of your feet, on the day when I act, says the Lord of hosts.

Christians have always understood these words from Malachi as a prophecy of Christ's coming, a radiant new dawn. The promised dawn is personal. God comes in Christ as a person and he comes to find us as persons.

God wills only our good, and knows that we long for healing and restoration. When we honour and worship God, we find liberation from our past sins, from our present anxieties and from our fears for the future. Christ comes to set us free as individuals, societies and the whole human race. In the light of his coming, we see that wickedness is ultimately empty and self-defeating, mere ashes, to be trodden underfoot.

Meanwhile, as we wait, we prepare ourselves for the dawn by watching and waiting with the steadfastness of faithful sentries on the city wall. Prayer is perseverance. The sun will rise.

■ **PRAYER**
My soul is waiting for you, O Lord. In your word is my hope, for there is forgiveness with you. Therefore you shall be feared. Amen

Isaiah 49:3–4 (NRSV)

My cause is with the Lord

And he said to me, 'You are my servant, Israel, in whom I will be glorified.' But I said, 'I have laboured in vain, I have spent my strength for nothing and vanity; yet surely my cause is with the Lord, and my reward with my God.'

There is often a hard road to travel between the promise of God and its fulfilment. It is easy to become discouraged in our faith, to feel that our best efforts are in vain. But prayer is not a quick fix.

Faithfulness does not always reap a swift reward. The sense of effort being poured out to no avail can make us reluctant even to try to deepen our faith in God. Yet here the prophet will not let his own sense of discouragement deflect him from his calling. He is prepared to go on trusting, in spite of a lack of evidence that his trust is justified.

It is easy to believe, easy to love, easy to be faithful when things are going well, but when life refuses to conform to our wishes, it is sometimes hard to resist the negative voices in our heads. But that is when we most need to confront despair. It need not have the last word.

■ PRAYER

Help me to hang on, Lord, however long it takes. When I am weary, downcast, exhausted, I still lift up my soul to you, for you are my Lord and my God. Amen

Isaiah 51:12–13 (NRSV)

Why then are you afraid?

I, I am he who comforts you; why then are you afraid of a mere mortal who must die, a human being who fades like grass? You have forgotten the Lord, your Maker, who stretched out the heavens and laid the foundations of the earth. You fear continually all day long because of the fury of the oppressor, who is bent on destruction. But where is the fury of the oppressor?

These words were written to the Jews in exile. They were deeply demoralised and fearful of enemies far and near. Warfare, defeat and captivity had led them to lose confidence in themselves and in their God. God replies to their complaints, spoken and unspoken, in person. He is the one who brings comfort and strength: the *only* one who can bring comfort and strength because he is the creator and saviour of all. The whole world is in his hands. Human destructiveness does not subvert his purpose or ultimately prevent his will being done.

At times of fear, it sometimes helps to make our fears concrete, to list them and to look at them objectively. They may still loom large, but real fears are often less terrifying than imaginary ones. There is ultimately no need, and perhaps even no point, in being afraid.

■ PRAYER

Lord, you know my fears and my hopes. Help me to be realistic about both, trusting your goodness and holding on to your promises. Amen

Luke 1:78–79 (NRSV)

The dawn from on high

'By the tender mercy of our God, the dawn from on high will break upon us, to give light to those who sit in darkness and in the shadow of death, to guide our feet into the way of peace.'

These words are spoken by Zechariah, the father of John the Baptist, as he looks forward to the new age which is about to begin with the coming of Christ.

There are so many today 'who sit in darkness and in the shadow of death'. We only have to think of those weighed down by disease, oppression or injustice. Then there are those who sit in the inner darkness of mental illness, neglect or cruelty.

Believing that God wills the best for us is the beginning of a recovery of hope, and the energy that comes with hope. Trusting that God acts in Christ to renew our human dignity is a step to finding that dignity restored. And even if we feel we have no peace in ourselves, the promise of Christ's coming can stir us to believe that peace will come. His mercies are tender and forever sure.

■ **PRAYER**

God of our salvation, we wait for you with longing. Break through the darkness of our sin and despair, that we may see the light of Christ coming into the world, and, seeing it, may rejoice, and, rejoicing in it, may find your peace in our hearts and souls. Amen

Speaking and sharing good news with vulnerable, yet valued, members of society

There was also a prophet, Anna, the daughter of Penuel, of the tribe of Asher. She was very old... She never left the temple but worshipped night and day, fasting and praying. Coming up to them at that very moment, she gave thanks to God and spoke about the child to all who were looking forward to the redemption of Jerusalem.

LUKE 2:36–38 (NIV, abridged)

When Jesus was brought to the temple and after Simon uttered his famous prayer, Anna steps into the limelight and prophesies of the redemption of Jerusalem. It is from Anna that BRF's ministry – Anna Chaplaincy for Older People – draws its name. Anna spoke of redemption, hope and God's good plan.

It is this same hope that more than 150 Anna Chaplains seek to share with older people across the country. While the pandemic hindered face-to-face ministry, God found a way. One Anna Chaplain, Elizabeth, conducted mini services with one person after another by phone. She read a Bible passage, sang hymns and offered prayers and thanksgivings. Many others found ways to continue ministering at this trying time.

Anna Chaplains help older people in care remain connected to other people and to those aspects of life which bring meaning and purpose to them.

Sustaining and growing this ministry is only possible because of generous donations from donors, churches, charitable trusts and gifts in wills. You can find out more at **brf.org.uk/annachaplaincy**. Please consider whether you or your church could support this ministry financially. You can get in touch with the fundraising team via **giving@brf.org.uk**, on 01235 462305 or by post. Your prayers, as ever, are hugely appreciated.

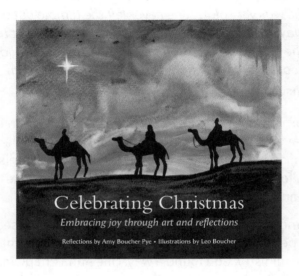

Celebrating Christmas
Embracing joy through art and reflections

Reflections by Amy Boucher Pye • Illustrations by Leo Boucher

Grab a cuppa and sink into a cosy chair as a father-daughter duo leads you into the celebration of Christmas through their art and reflections. Considering not only the story of Mary and Joseph journeying to Bethlehem, where Jesus was born, but also our modern-day expressions of Christmas, they bring light and life to what can be a fraught and exhausting season. A book perfect for giving as a gift or using oneself to foster joy and peace.

Celebrating Christmas
Embracing joy through art and reflections
Reflections by Amy Boucher Pye; illustrations by Leo Boucher
978 1 80039 051 5 £8.99
brfonline.org.uk

Introducing BRF's advocates lead

Jane Butcher has been BRF's advocates lead since September 2020. Jane is no stranger to BRF, having joined the team 13 years ago working with Barnabas in Schools and our Children and Families ministry.

As BRF seeks to further develop and celebrate volunteering across the organisation, one of Jane's key roles is to work with our volunteer managers to ensure all our volunteers have a rewarding and enjoyable experience with BRF. She also hopes to encourage more people to join us by raising awareness of our volunteer opportunities.

Jane is also gathering a team of volunteer advocates to share the work of BRF – our ministries, resources and support offering – in their local church and surrounding area.

Could you help or do you know someone who could?

Whether you have a little or a lot of time, previous experience of advocating or none, we would love to hear from you! We are looking for people of all ages who have a heart for what BRF does to help us raise awareness of our work and invite even more people to be a part of it.

All BRF volunteers can be assured of a warm welcome, ongoing support and appreciation as a valued part of our team.

If you or anyone you know might be interested in becoming an advocate for BRF, please email Jane at **jane.butcher@brf.org.uk**.

To order

Online: brfonline.org.uk
Telephone: +44 (0)1865 319700
Mon–Fri 9.30–17.00
Post: complete this form and send to the address below

Delivery times within the UK are normally 15 working days. Prices are correct at the time of going to press but may change without prior notice.

Title	Price	Qty	Total
At Home in Advent	£8.99		
Celebrating Christmas	£8.99		
Bible Reflections for Older People, January–April 2022 (single copy)	£5.25		
Bible Reflections for Older People, May–August 2022 (single copy)	£5.35		

POSTAGE AND PACKING CHARGES			
Order value	UK	Europe	Rest of world
Under £7.00	£2.00		
£7.00–£29.99	£3.00	Available on request	Available on request
£30.00 and over	FREE		

Total value of books	
Donation	
Postage and packing	
Total for this order	

Please complete in BLOCK CAPITALS

Title .... First name/initials .... Surname...

Address ....

.... Postcode ....

Acc. No. .... Telephone ....

Email ....

Method of payment

☐ Cheque (made payable to BRF)   ☐ MasterCard / Visa

Card no. ☐☐☐☐ ☐☐☐☐ ☐☐☐☐ ☐☐☐☐

Expires end M M Y Y   Security code* ☐☐☐   Last 3 digits on the reverse of the card

Signature* .... Date .... / .... / ....

*ESSENTIAL IN ORDER TO PROCESS YOUR ORDER

Please return this form to:
BRF, 15 The Chambers, Vineyard, Abingdon OX14 3FE | enquiries@brf.org.uk
To read our terms and conditions, please visit **brfonline.org.uk/terms**.

The Bible Reading Fellowship (BRF) is a Registered Charity (2332

BIBLE REFLECTIONS FOR OLDER PEOPLE **GROUP SUBSCRIPTION FORM**

> All our Bible reading notes can be ordered online
> by visiting **brfonline.org.uk/subscriptions**

The group subscription rate for *Bible Reflections for Older People* will be £15.75 per person until April 2022.

☐ I would like to take out a group subscription for .... (*quantity*) copies.

☐ Please start my order with the January 2022 / May 2022 / September 2022* issue.
(*delete as appropriate*)

Please do not send any money with your order. Send your order to BRF and we will send you an invoice.

Name and address of the person organising the group subscription:

Title .... First name/initials .... Surname..

Address...

.... Postcode ....

Telephone .... Email..

Church...

Name and address of the person paying the invoice if the invoice needs to be sent directly to them:

Title .... First name/initials .... Surname..

Address...

.... Postcode ....

Telephone .... Email..

Please return this form to:
BRF, 15 The Chambers, Vineyard, Abingdon OX14 3FE | enquiries@brf.org.uk
To read our terms and conditions, please visit **brfonline.org.uk/terms**.

ROP0321   The Bible Reading Fellowship is a Registered Charity (233280)

BIBLE REFLECTIONS FOR OLDER PEOPLE INDIVIDUAL/GIFT SUBSCRIPTION FORM

To order online, please visit **brfonline.org.uk/subscriptions**

☐ I would like to take out a subscription (*complete your name and address details only once*)
☐ I would like to give a gift subscription (*please provide both names and addresses*)

Title .... First name/initials .... Surname ....

Address ....

.... Postcode ....

Telephone .... Email ....

Gift subscription name ....

Gift subscription address ....

.... Postcode ....

Gift message (*20 words max. or include your own gift card*):

....

....

Please send *Bible Reflections for Older People* beginning with the January 2022 / May 2022 / September 2022* issue (**delete as appropriate*):

(*please tick box*)	**UK**	**Europe**	**Rest of world**
Bible Reflections for Older People	☐ £19.95	☐ £27.45	☐ £31.50

Total enclosed £ .... (*cheques should be made payable to 'BRF'*)

Please charge my MasterCard / Visa ☐ Debit card ☐ with £ ....

Card no. ☐☐☐☐ ☐☐☐☐ ☐☐☐☐ ☐☐☐☐

Expires end ☐☐ ☐☐ Security code* ☐☐ Last 3 digits on the reverse of the card

Signature* .... Date .... / .... / ....
*ESSENTIAL IN ORDER TO PROCESS YOUR ORDER

Please return this form to:
BRF, 15 The Chambers, Vineyard, Abingdon OX14 3FE | enquiries@brf.org.uk
To read our terms and conditions, please visit **brfonline.org.uk/terms**.

The Bible Reading Fellowship is a Registered Charity (23328